THE STORY OF *Barbie*™

AND THE WOMAN WHO CREATED HER

By **CINDY EAGAN**
Illustrated by **AMY JUNE BATES**

Random House New York

BARBIE and associated trademarks and trade dress are owned by,
and used under license from, Mattel.

Copyright © 2017 Mattel. All Rights Reserved.

www.barbie.com

Published in the United States by Random House Children's Books,
a division of Penguin Random House LLC, 1745 Broadway, New York,
NY 10019, and in Canada by Penguin Random House Canada Limited,
Toronto. Random House and the colophon are registered trademarks of
Penguin Random House LLC.

Page 26 watercolor brush lettering © Inna Moreva/Shutterstock

Visit us on the Web! randomhousekids.com

Educators and librarians, for a variety of teaching tools, visit us at
RHTeachersLibrarians.com

Library of Congress Cataloging-in-Publication Data
Names: Eagan, Cindy, author. | Bates, Amy June, illustrator.
Title: The story of Barbie and the woman who created her by Cindy Eagan;
illustrated by Amy June Bates.
Description: First edition. | New York: Random House Children's Books, 2017.
Identifiers: LCCN 2016048951 | ISBN 978-0-399-55378-3 (hardcover) |
ISBN 978-1-5247-7058-7 (lib. bdg.)
Subjects: LCSH: Barbie dolls—History—Juvenile literature. | Handler, Ruth—
Juvenile literature.
Classification: LCC NK4894.3.B37 E16 2017 | DDC 338.4/76887221092—dc23

MANUFACTURED IN CHINA
10 9 8 7 6 5 4 3 2 1
First Edition

My whole philosophy of Barbie was that through the doll,
the little girl could be anything she wanted to be.
—Ruth Handler, Barbie's creator

Ruth Handler loved to invent. She was always thinking of new ideas for fashionable jewelry and dollhouse furniture.

One day, Ruth noticed that her daughter, Barbara, didn't play with her baby doll. These were the only kind of real dolls that most girls had during this time. Instead, she was creating stories using paper dolls that looked like grown-ups.

This gave Ruth an AMAZING idea.

"Let's make a doll who looks like a teenager with different clothes she can wear on her imaginary adventures."

No one else thought it was a good idea.
"IMPOSSIBLE!" claimed the designers at Ruth
and her husband's toy company, Mattel.

Hearing the word *impossible* only made Ruth more determined. She would find a way.

Ruth and her designers worked hard on the doll . . .

until she was just right.

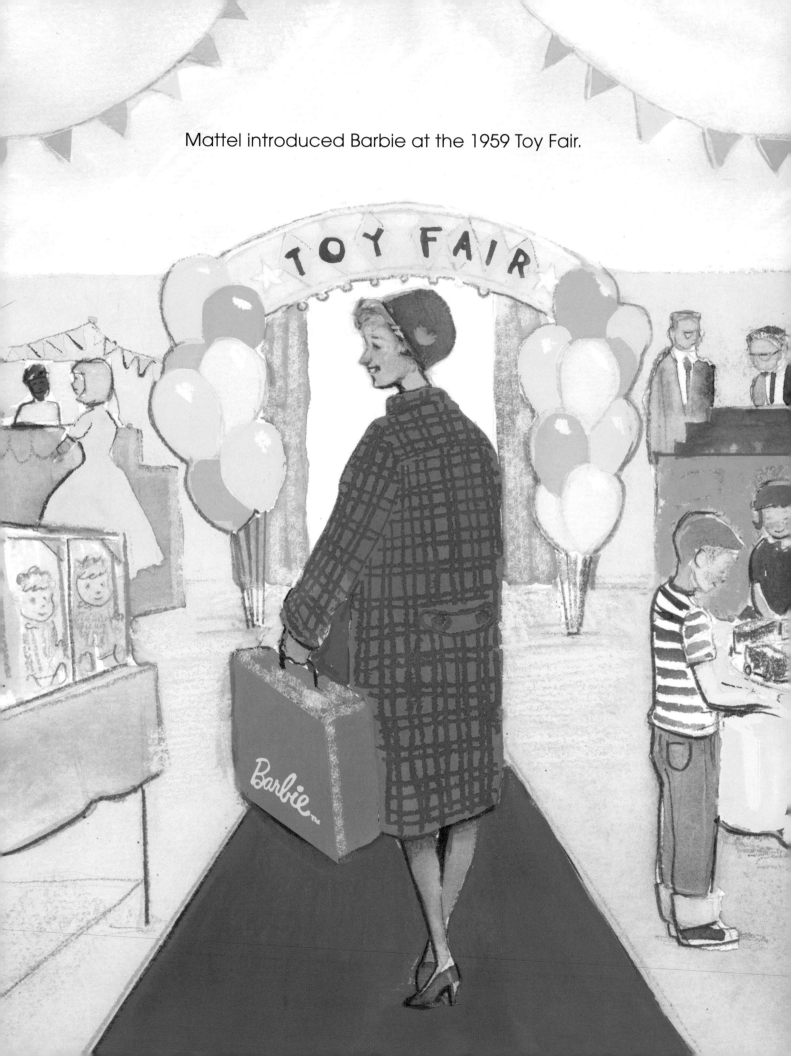

Mattel introduced Barbie at the 1959 Toy Fair.

Barbie: Teenage Fashion Model

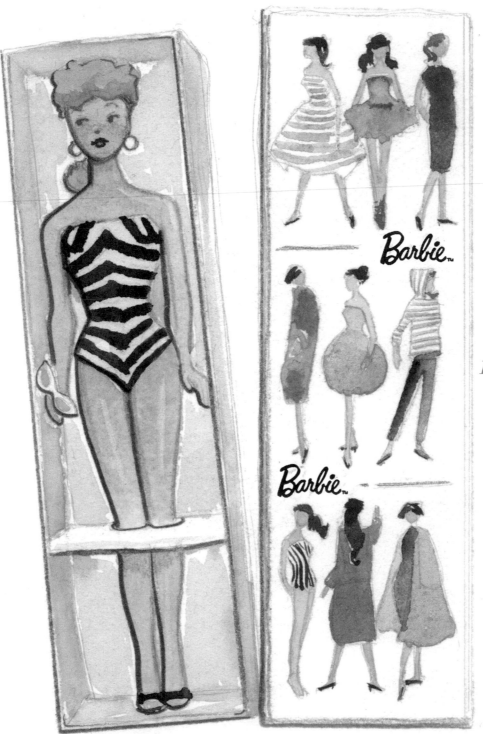

*Stands
11-1/2 Inches Tall*

*An Exciting, All-New Kind of Doll
(She's Grown Up!) with Fashion
Apparel Authentic in Every Detail!*

Ruth wanted Barbie's life to feel real. Her clothes, shoes, and purses were made with as much detail as possible.

Barbie sold out everywhere. Mattel raced to make more dolls while Ruth dreamed up Barbie's next adventures.

She decided to dress Barbie in clothes inspired by French designers.

Sparkly earrings, beautiful fabrics, sleek dresses with tiny buttons, coats with linings, and short white gloves: high fashion was now in reach of everyday girls and had never been so much fun.

Barbie's looks reflected the fashion of the time.
She was at the center of style.

Ballerina

Nurse

Singer

Flight
Attendant

As women became a larger part of the workplace, Ruth
believed Barbie should have jobs that girls dreamed of. They
could spend hours playing make-believe, imagining themselves
as Barbie and trying different careers with each outfit.

Soon Barbie's world would get bigger with
the creation of Ken . . .

her Dreamhouse . . .

and all her friends.

peace

As the world around her changed, Barbie did, too. Ruth kept pushing Barbie ahead.

love

groovy

Astronaut Barbie went to space four years before
the first real astronauts walked on the moon in 1969.

Whether she cared for her patients . . .

or competed at sporting events . . .

or served tea to a dinosaur ballerina,

Barbie represented all that was possible.

Ruth continued to pay attention to the shifting spirit of our nation.

Barbie's world reflected the world around us. She first ran for president in 1992 and has run five more times since.

Ruth Handler's influence lives on in Barbie's legacy. Ruth persisted when others said her dream was impossible. She created a doll to inspire girls to imagine their future.

Barbie continues to encourage girls to
be anything they want to be.

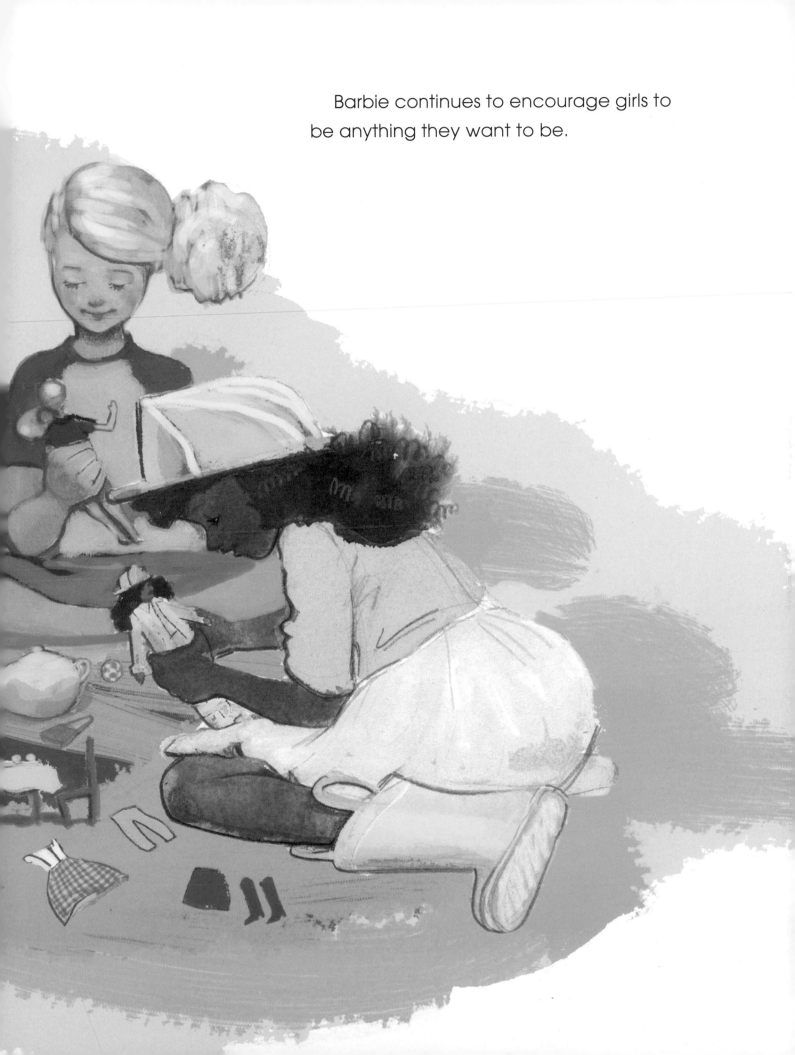

Who will she be next?

That's up to YOU!